HOW DOES GPS WORK?

Leon Gray

Published in paperback in 2016
First published in hardback in 2015
Copyright © Wayland 2015

Wayland
An imprint of
Hachette Children's Group
Part of Hodder & Stoughton
Carmelite House
50 Victoria Embankment
London EC4Y 0DZ

Produced for Wayland by Calcium
Design by Simon Borrough

Picture Acknowledgements:
Cover: Shutterstock: Boris Rabtsevich. Inside: Dreamstime: Anthonyata
45, Viorel Dudau 44l, William Attard Mccarthy 14, Niek 40, Tyler Olson 29b,
Robert Reyl 41, Photomo 36, Stocksolutions 43, Synchronista 42; NASA 7,
13r; Shutterstock: Am70 25, Auremar 30, Tony Bowler 27, Bplanet 5b, Rob
Byron 12, Cheryl Casey 37, ChameleonsEye 16, Ekkachai 1, 19, R. Fassbind
29t, Paul Fleet 17, Peter R. Foster 18, Germanskydiver 28, Guentermanaus
32, Patricia Hofmeester 33, Hxdbzxy 23t, Amy Johansson 23b, KPG Payless
34, Daryl Lang 38, Lithiumphoto 4, Rafal Olechowski 3, 22, Oorka 6, 10,
Pincasso 5t, Patrick Poendl 35 Scott Prokop 31, Nicholas Rjabow 9, Henryk
Sadura 8, Salajean 26, Dr Ajay Kumar Singh 24, Carolina K. Smith 20,
Spotmatik 44r, Jordan Tan 15, Tomas1111 39; Wikimedia Commons: Cadmio
13l, David Monniaux 11, United States Air Force 21.

A catalogue record for this book is available from the British Library

ISBN: 978 0 7502 9066 1
Printed in China
10 9 8 7 6 5 4 3 2 1

FSC
www.fsc.org

MIX
Paper from
responsible sources
FSC® C104740

An Hachette UK company
www.hachette.co.uk
www.hachettechildrens.co.uk

CONTENTS

CHAPTER ONE

WHAT IS THE GPS?

The Global Positioning System (GPS) is a network of high-tech satellites that allow people to find their position anywhere on our planet. Anyone with a GPS receiver can pick up the signals from these satellites to pinpoint their location on Earth.

Separate segments

The GPS consists of three parts or segments. The 'space segment' is the network of satellites that zooms around in space, thousands of kilometres above Earth's surface. These satellites beam radio signals down to our planet and connect with the 'user segment' – anyone with a GPS receiver. Finally, the 'control segment' is the part that maintains the satellites in orbit around Earth.

From the United States

The GPS is a US invention. Scientists developed it for military forces. The GPS helps soldiers find their way in unfamiliar territory and allows military commanders to plan their operations. It also guides missiles to their targets.

A hiker uses a handheld GPS device to fix his position on a mountain pass.

A driver enters an address into a touch-screen sat-nav system to find the way to her destination.

The driver can follow the route using a map displayed on the screen of the sat-nav system.

GREEN STREET

NORTH DUMM

GPS MAP
EPS10 : VECTO

RED STREET

SAMPLE TOLLWAY

G F

GPS for all

In 1983, the US government made the GPS available for everyone to use. At first, public GPS signals were made weaker than military signals and the public GPS was not very accurate. This changed in 2000, when the US government stopped making public signals weaker. Almost overnight, the GPS became much more accurate for all users.

Finding your way

Today, anyone can pinpoint their location on Earth and find their way around using a GPS-enabled device. GPS receivers are built into many electronic gadgets, ranging from smartphones to car navigation systems. Let's find out more about the technology that makes the GPS work.

BEFORE GPS

Before the GPS became available for everyone, people used paper maps and road signs to find their way around. And before then, people navigated using a compass, natural landmarks or the position of the sun and stars in the sky.

HOW GPS WORKS

The GPS is a series of 27 satellites, which spin around Earth in space. These satellites send radio signals to GPS receivers on Earth. In this way, the GPS satellites can track the movement of objects anywhere on the surface of our planet.

A GPS satellite orbits Earth. Two solar panel 'wings' trap energy from the sun and convert it into electricity to power the satellite's systems.

Satellites in space

Each GPS satellite is about 5.5 metres (18 ft) long and weighs about 1.3 tons (1.5 t). The satellites travel about 19,300 km (12,000 miles) above Earth's surface at speeds of up to 14,000 km/h (9,000 m/h). It takes each satellite about 12 hours to make one complete journey, called an orbit, around Earth.

Solar power

GPS satellites have huge solar panels to trap the energy from the sun. These panels extend out from the satellite like two wings, each measuring about 5.5 m (18 ft) long. Light-sensitive cells on the solar panels convert light energy into electricity. This is then used to power the satellite systems and send radio signals back down to Earth. The satellites also have nickel-cadmium batteries as a backup power supply.

A gigantic Delta rocket launches a GPS satellite into space.

SATELLITE SPARES

At any one time, there are 24 active GPS satellites orbiting Earth. The remaining three are spares in case one of the others fails. In the past, each satellite was built to last for about ten years but today's improved satellites have a lifespan of about 15 years.

Satellite launches

New satellites are built and launched to replace the worn-out satellites. Altogether, more than 65 GPS satellites have been launched into space. Some of the latest GPS satellites were launched from Cape Canaveral in the United States in 2014. Each satellite is reported to have cost US$245 million to build.

SENDING SIGNALS

GPS satellites beam radio signals to receivers on Earth's surface. These signals give information about the satellite's position. Each satellite carries an atomic clock, which shows what time the signals were sent.

Satellite signals

GPS satellites transmit radio signals at regular intervals. The atomic clock on the satellite ensures the signals are synchronised. This means that each satellite sends the signals at exactly the same time.

Speed of light

The signals travel at the same speed. They zoom through space at the speed of light, which is more than 300,000 km/s (186,000 miles/s). However, each GPS signal arrives at a receiver on Earth at a slightly different time. This is because some satellites are further away from the receiver than others.

The GPS antenna of a cell tower site (top left) picks up the signals from a GPS ground station to route mobile phone calls.

A ground station satellite dish picks up the radio signals from GPS satellites orbiting thousands of kilometres above Earth's surface.

EYES IN THE SKY

Scientists control the orbit of each satellite so that at least four satellites are 'visible' in the sky at any one time. The satellites have small booster rockets so they can adjust their orbit when necessary.

Calculating the position

Back on Earth, to calculate the receiver's position, the GPS receiver (which, for example, could be a handheld device, a smartphone or a car's GPS system) detects signals from four of the GPS satellites. The receiver then calculates the distance to each of the four satellites by measuring how long it took for the signal to reach it. The time difference between radio signals from four satellites is compared and then, using advanced maths, the GPS receiver can calculate its exact position on Earth.

MATHS LESSON

A GPS receiver does some very smart mathematics to work out its position on Earth. This calculation is called trilateration. The best way to understand trilateration is to picture it on a flat surface rather than in 3D space.

Reference points

Imagine you are lost. You need reference points to find out where you are. The first reference, point A, is 100 km (62 miles) away from your location. To work out where you are, you will need to use a scale of 1:10 so that each centimetre on paper is equivalent to 10 km (6.2 miles) on Earth.

Take a compass and draw a circle with a radius of 10 cm (3.9 in) to represent the 100 km (62 miles) around point A. You know you are at some point on the circumference.

Crossing circles

The second reference, point B, is 50 km (31 miles) away from your location. Draw another circle around point B with a radius of 5 cm (2 in) to represent the 50 km (31 miles). You must be at one of the two points where the circles meet.

Trilateration works using the reference points from three or more GPS satellites. Where the circles intersect, marks your position on Earth.

Third circle

The third reference, point C, is 60 km (37 miles) away from your location. Draw a third circle around point C, with a radius of 6 cm (2.3 in) to represent the 60 km (37 miles). The circumference of this circle will pass through only one of the points where the first two circles meet. You have just found out where you are!

Three dimensions

Trilateration works in the same way in 3D as it does on a flat surface, but the circles are spheres that overlap.

This GPS receiver with an external antenna is used to fix the user's position on Earth.

CHAPTER TWO

GPS AND THE MILITARY

The GPS started life in the 1960s as a military technology. It developed out of an arms race between the United States and the Soviet Union. Today, military forces use GPS technology for missile guidance, search and rescue and enemy surveillance.

The first satellite

In 1957, scientists from the Soviet Union sent the world's first satellite, *Sputnik 1*, into orbit around Earth. This was a huge achievement but it was also cause for concern. At the time, the United States and the Soviet Union were enemies. The United States believed that the Soviets were using *Sputnik 1* to spy on them.

Modern fighter jets are equipped with GPS-guided missiles to ensure they hit their targets.

The Soviet *Sputnik 1* spacecraft was the first satellite to be launched into Earth's orbit.

Satellite spies

The United States decided to keep an eye on the Soviet satellite. They used powerful computers to follow *Sputnik 1* as it orbited Earth. US scientists then decided to use the same technology to build their own satellites to spy on the Soviets from space.

The United States launched its first satellite, *Jupiter 1*, into space in January 1958.

SOUTH KOREAN DISASTER

At first, the GPS could be used only by the military. Then, in 1983, President Ronald Reagan decided to make the GPS for available for everyone to use. His decision followed an attack on a South Korean passenger aeroplane shot down by Soviet jets, killing all on board. The South Korean aeroplane may not have strayed into Soviet airspace if the crew had had GPS navigation.

The Cold War

During the 1960s, the conflict between the Soviet Union and the United States was growing. This period in history is called the Cold War. Both countries built nuclear weapons and threatened to use them against each other. In the following decades, the US government spent billions of dollars on satellite technology. This improved satellite system became known as the GPS.

FINDING THE WAY

GPS technology played a vital role in the success of the Gulf War (1990–1991). US military forces led the campaign in response to Iraq's invasion of neighbouring country Kuwait. Today, most modern military operations rely on GPS technology.

Desert directions

GPS technology was extremely useful during the Gulf War because the region is so desolate. Soldiers carried handheld GPS receivers to navigate in the deserts, where there were few landmarks to guide them. Using GPS technology, soldiers could also navigate in poor visibility, for example, at night or during violent sandstorms common in the region.

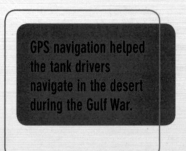

GPS navigation helped the tank drivers navigate in the desert during the Gulf War.

An inertial guidance system coupled to a GPS receiver will guide these Joint Direct Attack Munitions (JDAM) bombs to their target.

Missile guidance

Another common use for GPS technology is missile guidance. A simple GPS receiver converts a conventional gravity missile into a precision-guided 'smart bomb'. Military engineers can preprogram smart bombs with the target coordinates.

After launch, satellite signals constantly update the missile with its location so it can home in on its target. Since smart bombs rely on computer guidance, they can be used in all conditions, for example, in poor visibility and at night.

Signal jamming

Satellite-guided missiles do not always successfully hit their targets. One of the main reasons for failure is GPS jamming. This is when a GPS jammer (see page 41) disrupts the signals the missiles need to stay on target. As a result, many weapons have a backup, such as heat-seeking infrared systems.

FRIENDLY FIRE

The GPS not only provides an accurate position but it can also help distinguish friendly soldiers from enemy troops. Military GPS receivers send out signals to identify soldiers in combat zones. This reduces incidents of friendly fire (when troops fire on their allies).

SPY IN THE SKY

One of the main military uses of the GPS is for surveillance. GPS satellites orbit thousands of kilometres above Earth's surface, so they can be used to spy on people without them even knowing!

A Black Hawk helicopter evacuates soldiers from combat. The pilots rely on GPS navigation to coordinate the evacuation.

Military monitoring

The GPS is useful because it can pinpoint your location almost anywhere on the planet. The same technology can also tell you the location of others. Military commanders use GPS surveillance to chart the movements of enemy troops as well as monitor the position of their own forces.

Tracking troops

US military commanders first used GPS satellite surveillance during the Gulf War. Using GPS, they could track soldiers and their vehicles in real time, making it much easier to deploy their forces in the right places. In 1994, the US military developed a portable GPS-based tracking system called the Truth Data Acquisition, Recording and Display System (TDARDS). This system uses a computer, GPS data and a radio link to provide military commanders with accurate data on the position of aircraft, troops and ground vehicles.

A combat drone flies over the mountains of Afghanistan. Pilots on the ground can control the drone using advanced GPS navigation.

Behind enemy lines

Military GPS surveillance relies on troops working behind enemy lines. The soldiers use GPS systems to fix enemy positions on the ground. The troops then report the coordinates back to base so that military commanders can use the data to prepare ground assaults. The coordinates can also be used to program precision-guided weapons.

BLUE FORCE TRACKING

The US military and its allies use a GPS system called Blue Force Tracking (BFT) to provide the location of friendly and hostile military forces. The system also records conditions on the battlefield, such as the location of mines. Soldiers plot data on a computerised map and the system shares this with other troops in the area.

SAVING LIVES

In the combat zone, carrying a GPS receiver can mean the difference between life and death. Using the GPS, it is much easier to pinpoint the location of lost or wounded soldiers. Rescue teams use the GPS coordinates to speed up the search, which increases the chances of survival.

A Westland Lynx helicopter pilot relies on advanced GPS navigation systems to locate the position of a wounded soldier.

Military grid

Military GPS units map Earth's surface as a grid of squares, each measuring 10 km (6 miles) by 10 km (6 miles). This grid is called the Military Grid Reference System (MGRS). Each square on the grid is given a letter and number. For example, the square covering Chicago in the United States is called '16TDM'. The precise location of an object within each square is written as a ten-digit coordinate. These coordinates are accurate to within 1 metre (3 ft), which improves the chances of finding the casualties.

CSEL

Since 2005, a GPS-enabled device, called the Combat Survivor Evader Locator (CSEL), has been used by military troops. Soldiers in distress can activate the CSEL to transmit their exact location to search-and-rescue services. The soldiers can also exchange information, such as the state of their injuries and the position of enemy troops, making the rescue mission much safer and easier. Should the CSEL fall into enemy hands, the data can be erased.

Aircraft safety

All military vehicles have built-in GPS receivers to reveal their position all the time. This is particularly important for aircraft operating in combat zones, because there is always the chance that they will be shot down by enemy fire. GPS tracking helps to reduce the time it takes to find downed aircraft because the GPS data provides a record of the aircraft's last known location, speed, altitude and direction.

GPS technology is used by soldiers to carry out search and rescue operations behind enemy lines.

MODERN GPS

The GPS is no longer a technology used only by the military. Today, GPS technology is a common feature of many everyday devices that are used by people around the world.

Newspapers reported the death of Osama Bin Laden in 2011. US special forces soldiers used GPS technology to locate the terrorist.

Selective availability

At first, the US military did not want to share the GPS. Military chiefs believed that hostile countries and terrorists would use the new technology against the United States. When the US government opened up the GPS to everyone, it made the public signals much weaker than the military signals. This built-in error was called Selective Availability.

Time delay

With Selective Availability on, the time signal sent by each GPS satellite was not exactly the same. Without knowing this information, the GPS receiver on Earth could not provide a precise location. As a result, Selective Availability made public GPS signals much less accurate than military signals.

A space systems operator controls the constellation of GPS satellites that provides navigation data to military and civilian users.

Modern GPS

In 2000, the US Department of Defense stopped using Selective Availability on public GPS signals. The GPS then became more accurate for everyone to use. As a result, GPS receivers became a part of many gadgets, from smartphones to vehicle sat-nav systems, giving the public a chance to use military technology in their everyday lives.

SIGNAL ACCURACY

Today, the accuracy of GPS signals from space is exactly the same for both civilian and military systems. However, civilian signals broadcast over one radio frequency, while military GPS use two. Using two frequencies increases the accuracy of the military GPS by making the radio signals clearer.

CHAPTER THREE

GPS NAVIGATION

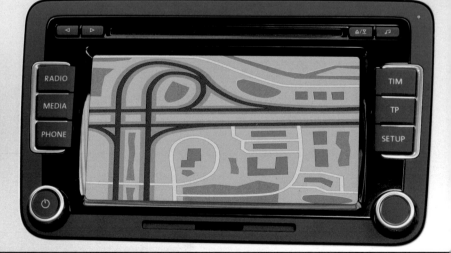

Many modern vehicles have built-in GPS sat-nav systems.

Ever since the US government made the GPS available to the public, companies have come up with more and more ways to use this technology. One of the main uses is to help people find their way around. GPS navigation is now common in applications ranging from air traffic control and in-car navigation to sports and games such as geocaching.

Satellite navigation

One of the first GPS success stories is for vehicle navigation. GPS navigation is now a standard feature of modern cars. These systems are called sat-nav, which is short for satellite-navigation.

On the road

Sat-nav systems help drivers plan the best route for their journey. They work by using the GPS signals to fix the position of the vehicle on a computerised map, which is stored on a database on the device. The map displays the car's position and the route. The driver can follow the instructions on the screen.

Aeroplane pilots rely on GPS technology for safe landings.

Easy to use

Sat-nav systems are easy to use. Drivers enter an address, landmark, or post code, and the sat-nav system plans the best route to guide them to their destination. Most systems have touch screens to make them easier to use when driving. Many include extra information, such as nearby service stations and restaurants. Some even speak to the driver using prerecorded voice commands.

Sat-nav problems

Sat-nav systems have many benefits over traditional maps. However they also have disadvantages. Drivers can take wrong turns if the maps on the device are out of date. It is important to update the maps to include road closures and other changes. Another disadvantage is that drivers can get lost if they do not check to make sure that their end destination matches the one to which the sat-nav is sending them.

AIR TRAFFIC

The Next Generation Air Transportation System (NextGen) is transforming air traffic control. NextGen relies on GPS signals to broadcast the precise location of aircraft in the sky and on runways. NextGen allows aeroplanes to fly closer together and avoid delays caused by 'stacking' as planes wait to land on an open runway.

Air traffic controllers use GPS technology to pinpoint the precise location of aeroplanes at take-off and landing.

THE GPS AT WORK

Many different industries use the GPS in the workplace. These include construction, where the GPS is used to aid the precise movement of heavy-duty machinery. There are also benefits in the open ocean, where navigation is difficult.

Earth-moving operations rely on the precise coordinates provided by GPS equipment.

Construction machinery

Heavy-duty construction machinery often comes equipped with GPS guidance to aid precision movement. It is even possible to use the GPS to preprogram the coordinates of foundations and other structures before the construction starts. The accuracy of the GPS means construction workers can move a load into exactly the right position.

Navigation at sea

In the past, sailors relied on maritime charts and complex calculations to navigate on the open ocean. Today, they can use GPS technology to pinpoint their exact position, speed and direction of travel, to ensure they arrive at their destination. GPS technology also helps sailors navigate through busy ports and waterways.

Fishing frenzy

GPS technology helps fishing vessels locate the best fishing areas. Programming the coordinates into the GPS device means the vessel can return to the same spot again and again. Some GPS devices combine GPS and sonar technology to recreate maps of the ocean floor. These charts can reveal features such as underwater trenches, which provide ideal hiding places for large shoals of fish.

SITE MAPS

In construction, the GPS helps engineers build accurate site maps. They create an electronic map of the construction site and feed in data from the GPS system. In this way, workers on the site can see exactly how far they are digging by comparing the depth of the hole with the information on the site map.

GPS technology helps fishermen navigate in the open ocean and locate prime fishing spots.

GPS IN SPORT

GPS technology can also be used as a training aid to increase performance in many different sports, from cycling and mountain biking to marathon running. GPS receivers are cheap, light and small, and they have also been built into devices as small as smartphones and watches.

Many recreational hikers rely on GPS technology for accurate navigation in unfamiliar terrain.

Fitness first

GPS technology has become a useful training tool for athletes. GPS devices can record the distance covered, time spent exercising and average speed reached during training. The data can then be downloaded onto a computer to assess performance and fitness.

GPS apps

Some companies have developed apps that use GPS technology to record training sessions. Strava is an app that has become popular with cyclists and runners. The app uses GPS technology to record how quickly an athlete can ride or run a section of a course. The athlete uploads the data onto the Strava website and can then see how he or she has performed against other athletes.

Shrinking in size

The first GPS receivers were large and heavy to carry around, which was not ideal for mountaineers or hikers on a long trip. Today, GPS receivers have been built into devices as small as watches. Innovations such as surface mount technology (SMT) and robotic assembly have shrunk GPS receivers onto tiny circuit boards so they can fit into smaller and smaller spaces.

HIT THE GREEN

Many golfers rely on the GPS to improve their game. They use GPS receivers to work out how far they have hit the ball and how far it is to the green. This information helps them select the right club for each shot.

Some golfers use GPS receivers to measure the distance from their ball to the green.

GPS FOR FUN

Some people have developed games that make use of GPS technology. One game is called geocaching. This treasure-hunting game uses GPS to locate containers, called geocaches, which are hidden by other players.

Skydivers use GPS receivers to measure their altitude as they fall to the ground.

Treasure hunt

People playing geocaching use GPS-enabled devices such as smartphones and GPS receivers. They use the GPS to navigate to a set of coordinates and then find the hidden geocache at that location. Most geocaches are simply a waterproof box containing a logbook. Players then sign the book to show they have found the 'treasure'. Some people hide more valuable items, such as books and toys. One of the rules of geocaching says that if you take an item from the geocache, you must replace it with something of equal or greater value. This means that the next person to find the geocache is not disappointed with his or her treasure.

Hidden treasure

People have hidden geocaches all over the world. The treasure could be up a tree, on the side of the street or even underwater. Once the geocache is in position, the player posts it on a website such as www.geocaching.com. People use the site to find out about hidden geocaches in their area and head off to find them. When the player locates one, he or she can record the find in the logbook or on the cache page on the site.

People use GPS receivers to hide geocaches. They record the position of the 'treasure' on geocaching sites.

This girl has used a GPS device to find a geocache hidden in the forest.

GEODASHING

Geodashing is another popular GPS game. It involves teams of players using GPS receivers to find random 'dashpoints' as quickly as they can. The first person to reach the dashpoint wins the game for his or her team.

CHAPTER FOUR:
MAPPING THE WORLD

Before the GPS, people relied on traditional paper maps to navigate around the world. Mapmaking was a time-consuming process that involved weeks or even months of painstaking measuring and recording. GPS technology has made mapmaking much easier. People can now draw maps on the spot using GPS receivers, computers and traditional surveying tools.

Modern mapping

GPS technology provides the precise coordinates to plot modern maps with amazing accuracy. Since the data from GPS satellites is instant, surveyors can plot coordinates immediately. They carry the GPS systems in backpacks or on vehicles so they can collect the data as quickly as possible. They can then combine this data with the information from surveying techniques, such as trilateration (see pages 10–11).

Surveyors combine traditional techniques with modern GPS technology to make accurate maps of the land.

These researchers are using a GIS system to show all kinds of data for a specific area.

Multilayered mapping

Most maps are now stored as electronic files and they display everything from motorway routes to local services such as service stations and convenience stores. The maps display data as a series of layers. This type of map is called a geographical information system (GIS). Unlike traditional maps, a GIS displays all the geographical data about an area. Each layer represents one type of data, such as all the motorways or all the service stations in a particular area. You can turn layers on or off to narrow down what you want to see.

Map updates

One of the biggest advantages of GPS mapping over paper maps is that GPS maps can be updated regularly. This is important because the network of roads and motorways is constantly changing. It is easy to update a digital file on a GPS mapping system as new bypasses are built and lanes are added to existing roads.

MAKING YOUR OWN MAPS

People can now create their own maps using GPS receivers and web utilities such as www.gpsvisualizer.com. These sites collect the data from GPS-enabled devices to create maps of where you have been, plan where you want to go and some even suggest somewhere to stop off for lunch.

GPS ANALYSIS

Scientists use GPS technology to help them with their research. Some use GPS technology to measure the impact of human activities on wildlife and on the environment. Others use satellite data to study and map areas of historical interest.

Scientists use GPS technology to measure the extent of deforestation in the Amazon rainforest.

Saving habitats

Environmental scientists study the impact of human activities on the environment. They study the effects of industries, such as farming and mining, on certain habitats. They feed in coordinates from GPS data onto satellite maps to record the damage these activities are having on our environment. In this way, environmental scientists have mapped deforestation in the Amazon and the melting of the polar ice caps.

GPS receivers provide the exact coordinates for all the artefacts buried at important archeological sites.

Digging for history

Archeologists study the past by digging up historical sites that contain artefacts, such as bones and pottery. Before the GPS, mapping sites to record all the data took a long time. Archeologists used measuring tape to lay a grid over the ground to record exactly where they found each artefact. Today, GPS data provides a precise location for every object they find.

Saving wildlife

Conservationists study and protect endangered wildlife. One way to do this is to attach GPS receivers to wildlife in the form of collars or harnesses. These collars and harnesses are then used to track the animals in the wild in real time. This helps the conservationists plan ways to protect wildlife from danger and to learn more about the animals. Similarly, some people use the same GPS technology to track their pets so they do not get lost.

FOREST FIRES

GPS technology is also used to help protect the planet. In Australia, forest fires are a constant threat in the scorching summer. Firefighters fly over a fire in helicopters mounted with GPS receivers to map the extent of the fire. Then they can plan how to put it out.

CHAPTER FIVE:
GPS SAFETY

Most emergency services rely on GPS technology for search-and-rescue operations. By carrying a GPS receiver, search-and-rescue teams can identify the location of the person in distress and plan a speedy response.

Saving lives

GPS technology saved many lives following the Japanese earthquake of 2011. Emergency search-and-rescue teams used the GPS combined with satellite images to map the disaster areas and plan their rescue efforts. The earthquake destroyed visible landmarks, such as bridges and highways so the GPS was an ideal way to coordinate the search-and-rescue effort.

Weather forecasters can use the GPS to predict natural disasters. In 2011, an earthquake devastated Japan. Early warnings would have helped the local people to prepare for the disaster.

RAPID RESPONSE

Scientists from the US National Aeronautics and Space Administration (NASA) estimate that it takes fewer than five minutes to detect and locate distress signals using the Distress Alerting Satellite System (DASS). This system relays the signals to emergency teams using GPS satellites.

Around the world, coast-guard vessels carry GPS equipment to locate casualties in an emergency.

European GPS

Countries from the European Union (EU) are developing their own satellite navigation system. Called Galileo, it also provides a search-and-rescue function. The Galileo satellites are fitted with a transponder, which is a device that transmits and receives radio signals. The transponder transfers distress signals to rescue coordination centres, which will then initiate the search-and-rescue mission. At the same time, it will send a response signal to the person in distress to let him or her know help is on the way.

App aids

Most smartphones now contain GPS receivers. People who enjoy activities such as hiking and mountaineering use mobile apps such as ViewRanger to find their way around and to broadcast where they are at all times. If they end up in trouble, the GPS signal can lead the emergency team directly to their location. The system even works in remote places with no mobile phone signal.

NATURAL DISASTERS

Scientists use GPS technology to predict earthquakes and tsunamis to prevent the huge loss of life that often accompany these natural disasters.

GPS-equipped buoys may be used to predict the underwater earthquakes that lead to tsunamis.

Quake alert!

Japan has been hit by some of the most devastating earthquakes in history. In 2011, a massive quake devastated the country. Japanese scientists are using a network of GPS sensors called GEONET to measure the underground movements that cause these violent earthquakes. The GPS data can be used to predict the size and strength of the quake and also where it will strike.

Watching the waves

Scientists study GPS data from ships and ocean buoys to measure the underwater earthquakes that trigger tsunamis – giant waves that speed across the ocean. Sensors detect the forces that shake the ocean floor and set the tsunami in motion. The data is then used to measure the location of the quake and predict where a tsunami will strike.

Weather watchers

People who study the weather are called meteorologists. These scientists also use GPS sensors to predict the weather so that news stations and weather websites can provide the public with a weather forecast. They study the radio signals from GPS satellites as they travel through Earth's atmosphere. For example, the GPS signals slow down in moist air, which may suggest that a storm is building up.

HURRICANE HUNTERS

Meteorologists use the GPS data from special devices called dropsondes to predict hurricanes. They release the dropsonde into the eye of the hurricane and the GPS receiver broadcasts the speed and direction of the storm. This can help to predict where the hurricane will hit.

Pilots fly aircraft into hurricanes to deploy GPS-equipped dropsondes.

WEATHER RECON

P
R
O
P
E
L
DANGER

GPS technology is not just used for navigation, it can also be used to track objects and people, from delivery vehicles and buses and trains on public transport systems to criminals on their smartphones!

Companies such as FedEx use GPS 'fleet tracking' to monitor the progress of deliveries.

On the move

Many delivery companies use GPS receivers as tracking devices on their vehicles. Some units are data loggers, which simply record the movements of vehicles and store the data as an electronic file. Other devices are data pushers, which use a mobile phone to send, or 'push', the data back to a computer at the warehouse.

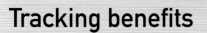
GPS tracking can be used to ensure freight trains deliver goods on time.

Tracking benefits

Companies use GPS trackers to check on the progress of deliveries so they can advise customers when they will receive their goods. This is called fleet tracking. The information from the GPS units can be used to check up on employees to ensure they are doing the job, too.

Public transport

Public transport networks use a similar system to fleet tracking to ensure bus and train services run on time. Computers track GPS signals from receivers on buses and trains and compare the location of each vehicle to the published schedule. If a bus or train is running late, the display can be shown to passengers waiting at the next stop. This way passengers will know when the bus or train will arrive.

FIND MY CRIMINAL

Apple's iPhone has an app called Find My iPhone that uses GPS signals to locate lost or stolen phones. In 2013, police in Queensland, Australia, managed to track and recover a stolen car because the owner's mobile phone was in the car and it had the app.

CATCHING CRIMINALS

Today's law-enforcement officers are turning to the GPS to help them catch criminals. They are using the information from GPS devices to provide evidence that could convict a suspect in court.

GPS tracking is playing an increasing role in helping to catch criminal suspects.

Surveillance

Detectives use GPS tracking devices and the data from vehicle sat-nav systems to follow suspects who are on the move. This can build up evidence about a person that may be useful in securing a conviction, for example, by placing a suspect at the scene of a crime.

Criminal conviction

The Metropolitan Police in London, UK, used a GPS tracker to convict a bicycle thief. The police fitted a tracker to a bicycle and left the bike on a side street in southwest London where bicycle thefts were high. When the bike was stolen, it was tracked to a well-known thief's house and then onto a further address. Police raided the second address and another 15 stolen bikes were recovered. Both men were arrested.

In a jam

Criminals are now wising up to the threat of GPS. They are using devices called GPS jammers to block the signals from tracking devices to avoid detection. GPS jammers are cheap and easy to buy, and some websites even show you how to build your own device. These jamming devices are effective because the signals used by GPS satellites are very weak.

SAT-NAV SUSPECT

In 2008, police in Chicago, United States, used the GPS data from a car sat-nav system to help convict a murderer named Eric Hanson. The police downloaded the GPS data from his sat-nav system to place him at the scene of the brutal murder of his family in 2005. Hanson was sentenced to death for his crime.

Detectives can use the information from vehicle sat-nav systems to place a suspect at the scene of a crime.

TAGGING CRIMINALS

Some countries are using GPS technology to monitor the movement of dangerous convicted criminals. They must wear GPS tags so the authorities can keep track of their movements.

GPS technology is providing law-enforcement officers with the hard evidence they need to secure criminal convictions.

Tagged

Criminals who commit less serious crimes can escape a jail sentence if they agree to wear an electronic tag. These tags broadcast the exact location of the people wearing them to the authorities. In this way, the police can follow criminals 24 hours a day to make sure they do not commit any more crimes.

Wearing tags

A GPS tag is simply a strong plastic strap that contains a GPS receiver. The tag is usually worn around the ankle and is almost impossible to remove. The GPS tag also contains a special circuit that, if broken by a particularly determined criminal, sends a signal to inform the police.

Rules of court

Sometimes a judge in court may impose certain restrictions on a prisoner who has served a prison sentence and is being released back into society. These restrictions may put limits on the time the offender is allowed to be out of his or her home – for example, a person wearing a tag may not be allowed out after 6pm and before 7am every day.

Exclusion zones

GPS tags can reveal all the information that a regular GPS receiver can show, such as the offender's precise location and the direction and speed he or she is travelling. The tags can also be used to enforce 'exclusion zones' to prevent offenders going somewhere they are not allowed to be under the rules of the court.

ABU QATADA

One of the first people in Britain to wear a GPS tag was Abu Qatada, a suspected terrorist with links to Al-Qaeda. Abu Qatada's tag triggered an alarm if he tried to leave his house without permission. In addition to wearing a tag, the court banned Abu Qatada from using a mobile phone, computer or the Internet.

The police always know the location of people wearing tags, so they are an effective deterrent against crime.

GPS ALL AROUND US

Until a few decades ago, the GPS was saved for military use. Hardly anyone knew about the network of GPS satellites circling high above Earth's surface. Today, it is difficult to imagine a world without the GPS. Who knows what the future has in store?

Stores now stock a range of GPS devices, such as vehicle sat-nav equipment. The price has fallen as the technology has become more common.

Many people enjoy recreational activities, such as sailing, thanks to GPS navigation.

Improving the GPS

The US government is spending billions of dollars upgrading the GPS. It is launching a new generation of GPS satellites to boost the signals and make the system more accurate. The United States is also working closely with European countries to ensure the GPS works with their new Galileo navigation system.

LOCATA

Locata is a new positioning technology. Locata uses ground-based equipment instead of satellites to send a radio signal over a certain area. This signal is about one million times stronger than a GPS signal, making Locata much more accurate and reliable than the GPS.

A GPS antenna on a remote mountain peak provides satellite communications over a wide area.

Location-based services

Most modern smartphones come with GPS receivers as standard. This has led to a huge range of GPS apps that are designed to improve our lives. Some apps use GPS data to suggest local services such as shops and restaurants based on where you are. Social media sites, such as Facebook and Twitter, are also using GPS data to help locate nearby family and friends.

Self-driving cars

As the GPS develops, people will use this amazing technology to change their lives in new ways. Sat-nav systems are already used to guide drivers to their destination. Future GPS devices may help cars drive without human control. All the driver will need to do is key the destination into the device and the car will drive itself there!

GLOSSARY

app short for application software, a program that tells a computer or other electronic device to do something

archeologist a person who studies human history through the discovery and exploration of remains, structures and writings

atomic clock an extremely accurate time-keeping device that uses the tiny vibrations of atoms to tell the time

circumference the boundary of a circle

conservationists scientists who study and protect endangered wildlife

coordinates numbers that represent the position of an object, such as a person, on Earth's surface

dropsonde a device used by meteorologists to study hurricanes

fleet tracking using GPS satellites to track delivery vehicles and buses and trains on public transport systems

geocaching a game in which players use GPS receivers to search for hidden treasures, called geocaches

Geographical Information System (GIS) a multilayered map that displays all the geographical data about an area on a computer screen

jamming using electronic equipment to block GPS signals

meteorologists scientists who study and predict the weather

navigation the process of finding out your location and following a route to a destination

orbit the journey a satellite makes around Earth

radio signals messages passed through the air in the form of waves of electromagnetic radiation

radius the distance from the centre of a circle to the circumference

satellites spacecraft that orbit Earth or another planet

Selective Availability the error introduced to GPS signals when the US government first opened up the system to the public

smartphones mobile phones that include high-tech applications, such as GPS, and an Internet connection

solar panels structures that contain light-sensitive cells that convert the energy from sunlight into electricity

sonar using sound waves to detect underwater objects or measure the depth of the water

surveillance spying on objects or people without anyone knowing about it

surveyors people who work out the position of things on Earth's surface

touch screens visual displays you can touch to control electronic equipment such as computers and smartphones

trilateration a mathematical calculation used to work out location by measuring the distances to known objects

tsunamis large waves caused by underwater earthquakes. Tsunamis cause widespread damage when they crash into the shore

FOR MORE INFORMATION

Books

Gray, Leon. *Ask the Experts: Global Positioning System: Who's Tracking You?* Franklin Watts, 2015.

Quinlan, Julia J. *How to Use Maps: GPS and Computer Maps.* Powerkids Press, 2012.

Sturm, Jeanne. *Let's Explore Science: GPS: Global Positioning System.* Rourke Publishing, 2010.

Websites

The award-winning How Stuff Works website explains how GPS receivers work at:

electronics.howstuffworks.com/gadgets/travel/gps.htm

The National Geographic website summarises GPS and its applications at:

education.nationalgeographic.com/education/encyclopedia/gps/?ar_a=1

Find out more about the European Space Agency's navigation system, Galileo, at:

www.esa.int/Our_Activities/Navigation/The_future_-_Galileo/What_is_ Galileo

INDEX